I0428203

KALEO

*

*

*

Flying High to Success

*

*

*

Weird and Interesting Facts on the Breakout Musical Group!

By Bern Bolo

Table Of Contents

***

Introduction

Hi, everyone! Here we are, once again, in Trivia Land where we provide information and random facts of some of the well–known artist of today with all interesting things that we can learn.

I'm so excited for today coz our topic of the day is a band! Yes folk, you heard it right, a band! I don't know about you but for me it's exciting. There will be different (or not so differences) people involved. What, why and how they come together is interesting.

Now, before we start we shall do the traditional game; The Game. I know that the name is not original but anyhow.

Ok, so our topic of the day, as I have mentioned, is a band. They originated outside of US and are making a huge splashed in the recent years. It is said that they followed the step of The Strumbellas.

With all of this information at hand, who do you think our artists of the day? Guess anyone? Hmm? Oh come on, the clues are all there!

Ok, ok. I give up. Our topic is the band called . . . Kaleo!

Now, let's go on and discover their amazing life. Kindly turned to the next page please. . .

Where We Came From

The band started as a jamming session or a hobby between friends in a garage. In a town called Mosfellsbær that was just outside of Reykjavik, the capital of Iceland, childhood friends JJ Julius Son, David Antonsson and Daniel Kristjansson loved music.

At the age of 17, they started playing, it led them to doing covers of various artists and performed live in pubs. They would accept all gigs they could find while attending school and as they say, the rest is history.

You must be thinking, what about the fourth member of their group? Where is he? Don't worry guys. He just came later in their life.

Rubin Pollock joined the trio last 2012. Rubin and David are mutual friends. David and friends decided to invite Rubin to one of their rehearsal. They have been together since then. That was also the time that they took their music more seriously and named themselves as "Kaleo". Kaleo is Hawaiian origin which means 'the sound'.

They jokingly mentioned at 90.9 The Bridge with Jon Heart that the only connection they have with Hawaii is David who was conceived there, which he admitted.

The then newly formed band performed at the 2012 Iceland Airwaves music festival for the first time. Kaleo performed in few shows that got positive responses.

In 2013, they started recording some of their songs like "Rock N Roller" and "Pour Sugar On Me". This got them attention in Iceland. Press and radio airplay was pouring. YouTube also was one of the biggest factors in their popularity today. Yes, I know that YouTube has the power to make you popular and in their case, it helped them got more exposure. Alright, I think I'm getting ahead of myself, let me tell you what happen.

They play a cover of an Old Icelandic ballad titled "Vor í vaglaskógi", which by the way is roughly translated as 'Spring in Vaglaskogur', in Rás 2, a live radio. The video of the said live was uploaded on YouTube and went viral. Their band was getting attention by more and more people.

See? That's the power of YouTube!

Later that year, during fall, Kaleo signed a contract with Sena, the largest record label in Iceland and released a full-length self-titled album and for only six weeks of making. They were stressed out, at the same time, learning something new since it was the first time to be in a studio. At least they were able to experience something new, right?

The album was a certified Gold and brought the band to shows and festivals all over Europe, including their home country. They made an appearance at the Culture Night.

"All the Pretty Girls" One of the singles of Kaleo was recorded last 2014 and the reason they garnered the attention of different managers, labels and publishers. The one that the band signed a contract with was the Elektra Records/ Atlantic Records Group.

It wasn't long after that and the quartet decided to move to the US, more specifically in Austin, Texas, as their new base, all these happened last 2015. The bandleader, Jökull Júlíusson (commonly known as JJ), admitted that it was a big change and a great adventure.

The American Dream

As what JJ said, it was a great adventure for the band. After signing with the Atlantic Records, Kaleo toured around the U.S. to explore possible music markets like Nashville. It was then that they all decided to move the pond. JJ said that all of them decided to move to Austin, Texas. The quartet mentioned that Austin's prosperity of American blues music and its history was a good way to use as an inspiration. The band admitted that they were fan of Delta blues from the 30's.

All of them lived in one house like a 'family', sharing rooms and such. Think about it, young men living on the same roof, doing what they want without restriction? I believe that's like a dream come true!

Lamberts, a local venue whose primary focus was blue music, was the first show visited after moving in. They slowly but surely got the attention of the citizen of Texas. Their biggest splash, however, was in South by Southwest (SXSW), the largest showcase festival in the world last March of 2015.

After that, they went touring with Vance Joy. The singer of "Riptide", remember? Daniel Kristjansson, commonly known as Danny, mentioned in an interview with the Huffington Post that this was their first tour around the U.S.

Their performance in SXSW on the other hand, gained the attention of magazines like Esquire's "40 Bands You Need to Hear" and National Public Radio's (NPR's) "The Austin 100: SXSW 2015 Feature and All Songs Considered SXSW 2015 Music Preview". That help their single "All the Pretty Girls" to snagged the #9 of Billboard's Adult Alternative chart.

After that, their songs were getting recognitions one after another. "No Good", which was released last 2015 and the first single of their second album, was the featured soundtrack on the HBO series titled "Vinyl".

The "Way Down We Go", which was released last 4th of October 2016, was used in movies, shows, trailers and advertisements. The song was the second single off their latest album "A/B" which climbed to the top spot on Billboard's Alternative Songs and Rock Airplay charts.

This single is the most famous out of all other songs the quartet produced and also the most talked about. The band performed the song inside the Þríhnúkagígur volcano. It was said to be the only volcano you can explore.

The third single "Broken Bones" was inspired by Alan Lomax's "The Land Where The Blues Began" (his memoir). The connection between segregation and slavery to Blues music was what inspired them to write their respective songs.

All three singles can be found in their second Studio album "A/B" that was released on the 10th of June 2016. The album got the #3 spot in Alternative Album charts and #4 in Top Rock Albums charts on 2nd of July. Of course, let's not forget their tours. They have been on multiple already.

Way Down We Go Tour, which featured Firekid, was their first tour. As you can see it's named after their own single. This happened in the early spring last 2016, February and March. This was followed by The Handprint Tour during the fall of the same year.

The second tour was so successful that they added more shows and dates for 2017. These dates were also sold out. Kaleo is also the special guest of The Lumineers on tour, their 2017 North America concert tour. They started last 28th of February through March.

As of now, we will wait eagerly for their tour and more amazing singles. Break a leg, guys!

Getting To Know You

Now that we've known them as a band, let's get to know them individually. Besides, they are four different people with different personalities, aren't you wondering how they got along? Well, now we don't have to wonder anymore!

Let's get to know their bandleader, lead vocalist, rhythm guitarist, and pianist, JJ.

JJ, whose full name Jökull Júlíusson, was born on 30th of March 1990. He is the one doing the composition of music. He started singing at the age of 17. The first thing he learned, related to music, was to learn piano, the classic one. After that, he started teaching himself and picking up songs. He also self-taught himself how to play guitar and singing followed.

But if you ask JJ, he would tell you that he was more of a songwriter than a singer. He mentioned in The Huffington Post that when writing songs, most of the time, the melody comes first and the lyrics follow. Most of the songs he wrote were personal.

For first time experiences, during the composition of "All the Pretty Girls", was the first time JJ sang in falsetto and learned how to whistle. Being a songwriter and a singer helped him develop his talents side-by-side.

Let's move on to little facts about JJ. In Metro Lyrics' My Musical Mind questionnaire, JJ mentioned that if he wasn't an artist today, he would be an athlete. He also mentioned that the very first album he bought using his own money was a Beatles record.

Next is Davíd Antonsson Crivello, the drummer.

Davíd Antonsson Crivello, or commonly known only as David, was born on 19th of August 1990. His family consists of 6 members, his Icelandic mom, his French dad, two brothers, a sister, and, of course, himself. He revealed in The Huffington Post that his musical talent runs in the family. His mother sings, his brother plays the guitar and his sister plays the piano, so he picked the drums. He met JJ and Danny from elementary school. They have been best friends since then.

David quit college early to help orphans in Egypt as a volunteer. Before he became a professional musician, he was a phone salesman, a car salesman, a travel agent, and a bartender. He had a very exciting life with the different kinds of jobs he had.

His hobbies are playing music - obviously, and snowboarding – wow!

In Metro Lyrics' My Musical Mind questionnaire, David wrote that if he wasn't an artist today, he would be a film director. It was either the AC/DC High Voltage or the Led Zeppelin 1 was the very first album he bought using his own money. The drink that he would like to have when they were in the studio was coffee. David also told them that the nicest thing that a fan did to him was a scrapbook filled with pictures and articles of their band.

The bassist of the group is Daníel Ægir Kristjánsson.

Daníel Ægir Kristjánsson, Danny Jones in short, was born on 1st of January 1990, making him the eldest in the band. His father was a former punk star in the 80's. I think music is in his blood too. He loves eating cookies and milk at 3 am (that's an interesting quirk), a lot of guacamole (it's an avocado dip or salad made by Aztecs which is Mexican) and margaritas.

In answering the My Musical Mind questionnaire of Metro Lyrics', Danny told them that if he wasn't an artist today, he would be a house painter. What an interesting choice!

Anyway, he also said that the very first album he bought using his own money was the Led Zeppelin II. What he would like to have when they were in the studio where good food and coffee. I'm guessing a pattern here. Giving Danny a bottle of vodka was what he considered the nicest thing you could do as his fan. I believe he's the one who drinks more in their group.

The last, but definitely not the least, was Rubin Pollock, the lead guitarist.

Rubin Pollock, luckily his name was not hard to pronounce unlike the others, was born on 7th of October 1990. They are all born in the same year. He was ¾ Icelandic and ¼ American, maybe the reason for his simple name. He was the last to join the band. They met due to a mutual friend. He likes eating cookies and milk at 3 am. If I didn't know better, I would think that Danny corrupt Rubin in this interesting little quirk (or was it the other way around?). Before he became a professional musician, he was a kindergarten teacher. Aww, isn't that sweet? He was a chess player too.

Of course, Rubin will not be left behind in answering the Metro Lyrics' My Musical Mind questionnaire. Rubin said that if he wasn't an artist today, he would be a sound engineer. It's not so far from his work right now. Utero was the very first album he bought using his own money at the age of 11. He loves relaxing and drinking coffee in the studio.

Aha! They all need caffeine when they're all in the studio. Though is it a curious thing why JJ like green tea more, unlike the others who likes coffee. For Rubin, showing up on their gig and buying their album was the nicest thing a fan could do for him. Ok, I will declare that he is the sweetest of them all. I don't know about you. But with all these information here, it will be your decision. But overall, I love them all!

Random Facts

Do you know everything about the band, as a group and as an individual now? Here's some more – here's the little facts and interesting quirks. Ready?

In 2013, Kaleo released an EP titled "Glasshouse". No more information about this, trust me, I looked everywhere. I am very interested to hear about this.

They have almost the same influences when it comes to music. Old Blues music, Classic Rock, and Soulful music, which when you think about it, is the main mixture of their music. It's not just one genre, they tap on different ones to make it more amazing.

And when I say amazing, it's with Capital-bold **A**. Anyway, let's go to the band members.

For JJ, he was acrophobia (in laymen's term scared of heights). But at the age of 16, he could bench press 140 kg (308 lbs). JJ was also a hockey player with Penguins vs. Flyers, in Pittsburgh, PA on 25th last February 2017.

David got something unique from a fan. Want to guess it? It was a painting.

Speaking of David, he shares a room with Danny on their tour bus. The reason? They both snore. I mean, really? But at least they can't disturb others!

Danny, however, has an aversion to bananas. I think 'aversion' is not as strong as what he had. He's more like deadly allergic to it. He can't eat the thing cause it will cause hives, swelling and wheezing. Just avoid that Danny!

Their single "Way Down We Go" became the featured soundtrack of FIFA 2016. Now this news is pretty awesome! Also, did you know that the song is one of their biggest success? It reached the #1 spot in Billboard!

References

http://www.billboard.com/articles/columns/chart-beat/7469309/kaleo-ealternative-songs-no-1-way-down-we-go

https://www.pri.org/stories/2016-06-10/icelandic-band-kaleo-taking-music-world-storm

http://www.officialkaleo.com/about

https://grapevine.is/culture/music/2015/05/19/kaleo-are-privileged-and-fortunate-play-the-blues-have-escaped-iceland/

https://en.wikipedia.org/wiki/Kaleo_(band)

https://en.wikipedia.org/wiki/Way_Down_We_Go

http://www.huffingtonpost.com/lauren-kruczyk/get-ready-for-the-sound-o_b_7182222.html

http://www.unofficialkaleo.com/kaleo-the-name.html

http://www.unofficialkaleo.com/meet-the-band.html

http://www.unofficialkaleo.com/jj.html

http://www.unofficialkaleo.com/tour.html

http://www.rollingstone.com/music/pictures/10-new-artists-you-need-to-know-february-2016-20160223/kaleo-20160222

http://www.altwire.net/2015/11/02/altwire-interview-kaleo/

http://popculturedaily.guru/kaleo/

http://www.metrolyrics.com/news-story-kaleo-my-musical-mind-handwritten-lyrics.html

Check Out **DUA LIPA's Trivia!**

Have you ever heard of a genre called "dark pop"? No? Well, me either. How many models turned musicians were able to succeed in the music industry? Maybe there were a few but I haven't heard of them! Did you know that she was a hostess at nightclubs? Of course, there is no such thing as smooth sailing life. Everybody encounters challenges and obstacles in life which is what makes you stronger and more motivated in the long run. Did you know that she was told that she can't sing 'cause she couldn't hit the high notes when she tried joining the school choir? I mean, isn't there medium or low notes in a choir? No need to let down the little girl so harshly? And she was really let down when she was told that. Who wouldn't? Did you know that when her manager told her that she needs to lose weight if she wants to be successful or want to do the catwalk, she stopped modeling because she loves food so much and instead she chooses to use the best asset she thinks she has which is her voice? I think both are her best assets. Her unique way of dressing herself up still portray her modeling days with her personal touch and her amazing voice as well! All these information and a lot more are inside -- so go ahead and take a peek, and then take one! If you're really into it, give them as gifts to friends.

Check Out DUA LIPA's Trivia

Get your copy of DUA LIPA's Trivia!

If you enjoyed this "Trivia", please leave an honest review on Amazon.com!

Sign-up here on Bern Bolo's site for Trivia On Twenty One Pilots!

www.ingramcontent.com/pod-product-compliance
Lightning Source LLC
Chambersburg PA
CBHW040318010626
45792CB00023B/1010